MW01137654

The Angled Road

by

Mount Holyoke College
Puget Sound Writers

The Angled Road
Mount Holyoke College Puget Sound Writers

Design by Roy Leban, Redmond, WA

Published in Redmond, WA

ISBN 978-1533010506

mhcpugetsoundwriters.com

Table of Contents

Cover art by Krista Lee Johnson '85

Foreword

Our writing group, the Mount Holyoke College Puget Sound Writers, had been talking about publishing a collection of our work for some time. "How will we choose which writings to include?" asked one person. "We need a theme," responded another. "Let's use one of Emily Dickinson's poems as the theme," said a third. We're all graduates of Mount Holyoke College; Emily Dickinson is perhaps its most famous alumna.

We selected "Experience is the Angled Road" as the theme poem. We then had an intense, three-hour discussion about what the poem meant — in essence, a Senior Seminar. While the poem means something slightly different to each of us, we agreed it spoke about change and growth in one's life as symbolized by the bends and turns of a road.

Growth and change was our theme. We would each write, or select from our existing pieces, those which embodied these ideas. (For a description of our process, please see the Afterword.) The pieces were read aloud to each other, and all agreed each piece fit the theme: describing personal changes that happened to us or to family members or friends, and how we became the people we are now based in part on these growth experiences.

Please read our theme poem thoughtfully. As you read the various pieces in this anthology, share with us the glory and struggle of life's journey.

—Jules Dickinson

910

by Emily Dickinson

Experience is the Angled Road
Preferred against the Mind
By—Paradox—the Mind itself—
Presuming it to lead

Quite Opposite—How Complicate
The Discipline of Man—
Compelling Him to Choose Himself
His Preappointed Pain—

Homecoming
by Teri Bicknell

It was still raining. Pink worms inched across the walkway that wound through the front yard from the fence to the porch. I had been using rocks and sticks to direct a small stream flowing through the lawn, digging a rivulet and placing stones along the edge. If I lay on my stomach on the grass, it was a real river with banks and a rocky shore. Grandmother watched me through the kitchen window, which she had been doing ever since I slipped out the gate that time to see if there was a letter from my Daddy in the mailbox at the end of the driveway, telling me when he'd be back to get me.

The brook on the other side of the house splashed and danced because of the rain, whereas normally it only trickled, flowing under a little bridge by the highway, and then joining the big river, hidden behind a wall of grasses and cattails. I knew this because one of my first days here I had followed it down the big hill from where Grandmother's house was, up high with a view of the road. I got in trouble for exploring, but later Grandmother took me to a park with picnic tables where the banks were grassy and you could watch the black water flow past, swirling in curlicues on the glossy surface. I wanted to put my feet in, but when I took off my shoes she told me no, that the water moved too fast and I might be swept away.

Rain splatted on the hood of my coat, but the whine of a siren in the distance was louder and I stood up to look. An ambulance raced toward the house and passed it, like a match car hurtling down a plastic track. Another followed behind it, and then a fire truck. They all parked with their lights flashing, and a whole bunch of them, wearing dark shirts and matching pants, climbed out and disappeared into the reeds. I could see a little because of being up on the hill, but I stepped onto one of the swings on the old swing set for a better view. Cars had started backing up.

The front door opened behind me and Grandmother came outside. "Get down from there," she said. "You'll fall and twist your ankle."

I didn't move. The traffic crept forward both ways. "I'm not going to fall," I said.

"There's no reason to be a looky-loo." She stood on the porch and waited for me. "You know the rules. Inside now."

"Just a few more minutes," I said.

"You have your reading and vocabulary exercises."

"Five more minutes. Please?"

She watched me, shading her eyes in the brightening light. It had stopped raining and the clouds were thinning. The air felt warmer. "He's not coming today," she said. "Perhaps next week or in two weeks. Not today."

I kept watching the road. I didn't want her to see my face.

"Five minutes," she said and went in, closing the door.

Grandmother didn't normally give me reasons for why I had to mind her. But on one of her Bridge club nights, when a lot of white-haired ladies came to the house and I watched the public TV station with the sound turned down, they sat around tables smoking cigarettes, listening to old people music on the Hi-Fi stereo console, and sipping from glasses with tinkling ice. Grandmother started talking about the little girl who had drowned the week before. Her family had been on a picnic at the river, and next thing they knew she was gone. Three days later, someone found her in a marshy bend. It had been in the news, Grandmother said. So I could guess why I had to stay inside the fence, even though that girl was five and I was eleven. Then she started talking about the mental hospital again, and I got up and went to my room. I didn't want to hear that talk.

The traffic was backed up on the road as far as I could see in either direction by now. I looked through the living room windows, at the mirror that hung over the couch and the vase of plastic flowers on the dining room table where we ate our meals. Grandmother was in the kitchen at the stove, her back to me. It was almost dinnertime. I let myself out through the gate and ran down the hill toward the mailbox, every step a hard jolt. Then I was on the side of the road, my chest smarting, my breath coming fast, jogging next to a caravan of cars.

Some had their windows down, and there were sounds of talking. Music came from one, a Rolling Stones song. Another had the news on. The announcer said the word "jumper." I ran faster on rubbery legs. I didn't know why I had to see what had happened, I just did. I came upon the last of the ambulances and stopped at a flat place, where the grasses were tamped down, a green carpet littered with muddy footprints. I walked across it toward an opening, a darkened hallway through the reeds, bright at the other end.

"Don't go in there, kid. You don't want to see what's back there!" someone yelled from one of the cars. But I had to make sure. I had to see. I didn't care about the consequences.

Inside the reeds, it was blackish green all around. The ground felt spongy and sank with each step. It smelled wet and dark and rotting. The sun had come out and the heat made the air steamy. My face was red hot, damp with sweat. My pants stuck to the insides of my legs. My feet were boiling. I pulled off my coat and thought, when I get to the river I'm going to put my feet in and see what it feels like. But by the time I reached the end of the tunnel, each footstep fell with a splash. I was in the river already. The water was cold, but I barely noticed.

Now I heard voices up ahead and there were eight or ten men, some in the shallow part that was normally the shore, not far from where I stood. Some in up to their arms, holding onto a tree jutting out, their bodies pulled sideways in the racing water, brown like creamy coffee. Two of the men held onto something else, dark and soaked-looking, like a log that had been wet a long time. Only it wasn't a log, it was a person, a man, face-down. They kept trying to maneuver him at the shoulders and the ankles, but he started floating away. Three swam out, holding a yellow rope. It took them a while, arms thrashing in the messy current, yelling orders to each other, and they brought him to a shallow place, a dripping rigid board. No one had noticed me, but then one of them did.

"What are you doing here? You shouldn't be here!" a guy in yellow overalls yelled with an angry face. "This is a crime scene. Get back to the road."

"A crime scene?" I said.

A whole bunch of policemen crashed through the reeds then, carrying radios and clipboards. One said, "How long has he been in the water? Where did he jump from?"

I knew what had happened then, and I had to see his face.

My Daddy wasn't a big guy, maybe five feet nine on a good day, and he wasn't a broad person either. Small jeans, small shirts. A small head of brown hair. He was normal. He was my perfect Daddy, not too big, and not too little either. Just like this person in the river, whose face I still couldn't see. But when they turned him over, something caught in my throat and I was almost going to cry because I thought it was my Daddy's face. But when they turned him a little more, I could see it wasn't him. It wasn't my Daddy. My Daddy had a mustache and a small forehead and a dimple in his chin. This person's face was pale and blown up like an ugly balloon. And maybe he did have a mustache, but I couldn't tell. I couldn't tell anything about him at all.

They turned him over, emptying his lungs. But it didn't do any good. He just shifted this way and that, like a mannequin. They lifted him onto a stretcher and covered him with a sheet, carrying him out. I followed behind. I didn't want to be there by myself. I didn't want to be there at all anymore. My feet felt slimy and gritty hot. I wanted to take off my shoes, but I had to keep walking.

When they moved out of the green tunnel, she was standing at the end, my grandmother, blocking the view of the ambulances and the people and the stretcher with her tall slacks and her turtleneck sweater.

Her eyes were shadows in the bright sun.

Walk With a Cane
by Jules Dickinson

Oh how you tried
To cut me down to size
By saying things to make me doubt my power.
And I believed you -
The dumb things that I do!
Internally I'd cringe and then I'd cower.

But now I walk with a cane
Rock with a cane
Dance with a cane, oh yes
My legs don't move much
But with work and luck
I'll dance with joy and finesse!

I must end the black
Don't want to feel the black
I tried razors, then a shotgun blast.
But when I didn't die
I decided not to cry
Choosing to live life, my crisis passed.

Now I walk with a cane
Rock with a cane
Dance with a cane, oh yes
Forget that bad guy
I'd rather live and fly
And dance with joy and finesse!

A bad and evil boss -
Your plan for me has lost.
What manager could do this to his staff?
If I were to think of you
I'd feel pity through and through;
Instead I live, I love, and I laugh.

Meanwhile I walk with a cane
Rock with a cane
Dance with my cane, oh yes
I'll tell the world
My life flag's unfurled
And I dance with joy and finesse!

I Live on the Edge
by Jules Dickinson

I live on the edge.
I like to drive the speed limit.
I use my turn signals, even in parking lots.
I check all mirrors, then look over my
    shoulder, before changing lanes.

I live on the edge.
I have no desire to sky dive.
I don't want to bungee jump.
I have no plans to parasail.

I live on the edge.
I won't go white water rafting.
I don't surf or windsail.
I avoid riding Jet Skis.

I live on the edge.
I don't gamble in casinos.
I don't day trade on the stock market.
I don't buy storage units at auction.

I live on the edge.
I visit my dentist regularly.
I see my doctor for a complete annual
    physical.
I take prescription medications according to
    directions.

I live on the edge:
I drink diet Pepsi
And
I eat raw cookie dough.

Jump
by Elizabeth Burr-Brandstadt

I was exhausted. I was leaving a book fair, after four days, and I was dragging a broken rolling suitcase full of journals and books behind me. The handle was broken, and the behemoth-on-wheels kept doing that thing where it flips without any warning, twisting my wrist and leaving me with a sudden thunk of weight and pain that completely undermined any joy I might have felt that I could finally go home. It was pouring rain outside, and I had an eight block walk to the train ahead of me. I was still trying to leave the convention center, waiting to get onto the escalator that was causing a bottleneck of anxious bodies trying to descend to street level.

To make matters worse, when I was actually about to step onto the escalator, I had a young family in front of me: mother on the phone, father coaxing along the wobbly two-year-old. "Pick him up!" I grumped to myself; I was in no mood to smile patiently at a gimpy toddler. "Jump!" yelled the father, "Come on, Buddy, jump!" The child looked at him, clung to the oblivious mother's hand, looked down again, and skipped onto the grated, moving stairs. He jumped! How about that? My anger completely dissipated; I was disarmed, and I smiled. I caught the father's eye, and said, "They're tricky, those escalators!" Dad made a face of mock fear and threw up some jazz hands; "The floor is moving!" he wailed. We smiled.

At the bottom, the little guy leapt to the finish line and then turned to the still-descending crowd. Throwing his arms in the air, he called out "Jump!" to no one and everyone. I felt so tender for this small person, who moments before had been afraid. Not of terrorists, or mortgage values, or from where his next meal was coming, but of being hurt. How was he supposed to know that this moving metal monster of sharp teeth and raw edges wasn't going to devour him, or at the very least take his shoe? And what sage advice he gave to the crowd. When you're stuck, just jump.

Out of my reverie and back to slogging along, I went outside where I intended to cross the street. I provoked the ire of a Jeep driver by stepping into a crosswalk with only a couple of seconds to spare, and he swerved within a few millimeters of my body, punishing me for carelessly wandering into the street. I faltered, but would have made it, if it weren't for the giant, woman-eating puddle. As I stood in the middle of the puddle (because when your choice is between getting wet and getting hit by a Jeep, you get wet), I realized that I should have remembered the kid's advice.

Eventually I reached the metro, pushed my suitcase into the area marked for luggage, and dutifully sat across from my soggy baggage. I revisited my exhaustion and misery, and made the conscious decision to feel sorry for myself for an unspecified period of time. But then, there he was: a wheelchair-ridden, pathos-inducing character regaled in Seahawks paraphernalia, who needed to slowly and painfully back into the reinforced area where handicapped people can safely travel. I had to move my suitcase for him. This was the part where I was supposed to have the revelation about how truly blessed I am, and reflect on my own physical prowess, but that's not what happened, because, as previously mentioned, I was mired in self-pity. In fact, I was jealous that he got to ride around in a chair. I bet the Jeep would have stopped for him.

Then a man sitting behind me, whom I had seen briefly because he'd dumped his damned backpack on top of my suitcase, spoke to the man in the wheelchair. Now, most people would tune in to the ensuing conversation with interest tempered by compassion, or at a polite distance feigning disinterest to protect the sensitive nature of its content. Not me. That guy, Backpack-Thrower, had put his bag on my suitcase despite the fact that I was clearly trying to maneuver a space for Wheelchair-Man. Sheesh.

"When did you have your leg amputated?" Backpack-Thrower asked. (Amputation. Why didn't I see that?)

"About a year ago," said Wheelchair-Man. "Diabetes."

A moment went by, and Backpack-Thrower said, "My friend had his leg amputated last month. Same thing, diabetes."

Finally, no talking, just the glide of the oft-jerky movement of the train. My self-indulgent misery was melting into something close to self-recrimination. I wasn't going to let everyone off the hook, though. After all, was everyone else wet? (Yes.) And tired? (Probably.) But it did occur to me that there were some problems, some pain, that couldn't be jumped out of or over.

Then Wheelchair-Man said, "Does it hurt?"

"What?" said Backpack-Thrower, a bit surprised.

"Your friend, does his leg hurt him where it was amputated?"

"Oh," said Backpack-Thrower. "It's taken some getting used to, but he's grateful to be given another chance."

Silence again. And then, finally, the question that needed asking.

"Sir?" asked Backpack-Thrower. "Does your leg hurt?"

"Yes."

I was right about not being able to jump out of pain. There is an anchoring, an inescapable heaviness of pain that holds us to the earth, forbidding a jump, or even a skip. Naturally, because I'm not the cold-hearted cynic you may have been led to believe, when the man in the wheelchair disembarked at my stop I asked him if I could help him from our elevated platform to the ground level, which coincidentally was on an escalator ("Trips on escalators lead to enlightenment!" I joyfully thought.). "Thank you," he replied politely, "but I know how to use the elevator." Oh. There was an elevator too. No jumping necessary.

Because I try to be a student of the world, and not a heartless wretch, I did learn that day about the privilege of being able to physically and metaphorically jump. In addition to this privilege, however, I must be more mindful of the gap between what I know intellectually, and what I fail to realize because of my experience. Sometimes I don't know a single thing about fear or pain. Heretofore, I hadn't thought at all about how it must feel to be so thoroughly grounded that you can't rise up, even for a moment. I should think about that fact, though, since, because of my academic interests and the Oxford English Dictionary, I know that the word "grounded" means that something that could be unfettered is suppressed, like a plane, or a wayward teenager. But it also describes someone or something that has a firm foundation, fixed in a way that protects its object from a lack of judgment or flights of fancy. I certainly would have done well on my journey that day to be a bit more grounded. After all, one doesn't have to take the escalator. There are elevators, and ladders, and stairs, and many ways to go up and down.

Upon even further reflection, I characteristically started berating myself. How dare I? A two-year-old knows that every day can draw blood. A fervent Seahawks fan in a wheelchair knows to ask about pain, and then share his own. And I had a bad day because my rolling suitcase was putting a strain on my carpal tendon. Then poor me had to get on the metro, which would, within a half hour, deliver me to my car, which I would then drive to my warm home. This disaster would culminate in a hearty meal followed by television-watching and curling up in a downy bed. Oh, the humanity!

But I think I'll give myself some leeway, here, because ultimately, I was able to come out of myself and learn something. Here's what I should remember from this rainy Saturday in Seattle: If you want help, ask for help, instead of complaining about the lack of sensitivity surrounding you. Ask others what it is they actually need, and not what you have determined will best serve them. Respect the experience of people who have been relegated to "less than" the norm, be they physically or mentally challenged (or two-year-olds, who are both). And while you are able, when the opportunity arises, elevate yourself however briefly to gain a new perspective, save yourself, or find a new joy. Jump.

Recovery
by Emily Dietrich

Not to succumb
To the downward suck,
Her efforts throw her
Across the magnetic
Abyss,
Safely settled
Only
Momentarily,
While momentum builds
In her iron soul.

Obeying her compulsion
Her next propulsion
An opposite motion,
Destination
Anywhere but there;
Goal?
Don't sink.
Roll.

Meeting
by Emily Dietrich

Prenatal

Tiny tightness,
Carefully crafted,
Manifests majesty—
Excellence exhibited
As an accurate agenda
Prepared, in place, perfumed—
Reaps rewards and recognition.

Post Partum

Eruptions, loosed,
Befoul the room
Idealism smearing the wall,
Pain speckling Styrofoam cups,
Rage melting plastic seatbacks, and

Sweaty compassion
Embracing each stutter,
Honoring burps and spittle

Fits
Starts
Rail against revulsion,

Reel toward self-respect.

Three Knocks in the Night
by Sue Swanson

It was a hot June afternoon in 1890. Outside the large mullioned window the fragrant roses and the soft green hills of western Massachusetts were lost on the two girls sitting stunned in their dorm room. Ida Scudder and Annie Hancock sat on the bed staring at the cable in Ida's hand. Ida, in her flowered muslin dress, a halo of fair hair piled on top her head and eyes so blue her family called her "Bonnie", was shaking her head in disbelief. Annie, small and intense, her brunette head bowed low with Ida's, re-read the cable. A ray of sunlight danced over their contrasting yellow and brown heads. The girls had just graduated from the Northfield School for Girls and were looking forward to a fall of college parties and dances, Ida at Mt. Holyoke College. This simple piece of paper in Ida's hand had changed all that. "I just can't believe it!" Ida gasped her eyes filling with tears as Annie squeezed her hand in sympathy.

Ida Scudder was a missionary kid. Her grandfather, Dr. John Scudder, the first medical missionary sent out from the United States, had sailed from Boston to Ceylon in 1819. Her father, John, also a doctor, and the youngest of seven missionary sons had been serving in India for thirty years. Ida had been born at her parents' mission in India but had been sent to the Northfield School for her education. Her reputation as the lighthearted instigator of pranks, and the most popular girl with the boys at nearby Mt. Herman School often landed Ida in trouble. Annie, quiet and spiritual, had fit in more easily at a school that catered to missionary daughters. The girls, as different in personality as their coloring, had been best friends and inseparable since their freshman year often discussing their religious views. "I will never return to India!" Ida had vowed to Annie, her blue eyes snapping. "I am not going to become one of those "Scudder Missionaries. Over thirty members of my family have already filled that role and they don't need one more!" The other girls admired Ida for being independent and determined. She had told no one about the recurring nightmares she suffered of the starving children she had witnessed during the terrible famine of 1875 when over 5,000,000 people had died. Ida had had enough of India. She wanted a normal life of fun, romance and friends.

Then the cable had arrived, "Come Immediately. Your mother ill and needs you." Ida had five brothers; as her parent's only daughter she knew there was no choice but to answer the call to take over her ill mother's duties as the wife of a missionary doctor. So, with a heavy heart, she took the next available ship to India.

The trip from the dock in Madras to the mission at Tindivanam was hot, dusty and miserable. She'd forgotten about the unrelenting sun, the cawing crows, the smells of incense and cowdung, spices and smoke. And the people! They were everywhere! Ida sighed and thought of the quiet cool hills of Massachusetts. At the mission compound the whitewashed bungalow her parents called home consisted of three small rooms in a row each one opening onto a long porch. The floor was packed mud with a layer of crumbled lime on top. White ants living in the thatched roof occasionally dropped onto the humans below. Ida hated it.

Sophia Scudder was recovering from malaria, but slowly. Her husband was often away visiting the

Christian congregations he had established in the villages of the area so Sophia had been left to carry on as mission manager and head of the boys' boarding school the couple had established. It was a lonely post.

"I see foreigners so rarely," her mother told Ida, "that when I had the chance to speak English last spring I talked so much that I spent the next three months repenting!"

"This life may suit you," Ida thought to herself. "but, it's not what I want. I'm going back to America and college as soon as you are well and can take over again." But there was no time to think about life back home. With guidance from her father, Ida threw herself into running the school and when he left again on a mission trip, the mission as well.

One evening a few months after her arrival, Ida was sitting in her hot, stifling room answering a letter from Annie. "I so envy your exciting life as a missionary," Annie had written. "I wish that I could also enter the foreign mission field."

"I'm not a missionary and never will be!" Ida had written in her reply, underlining the sentence with a fierce black line. "You are far more spiritual than I ever will be and you would probably like the missionary life. But I don't. It's not meant for me!" No sooner had Ida written that sentence when she heard a discreet cough (the gentle Indian call for attention) and a knock at her door. She picked up her lamp, went to the door and opened it. A young, dignified man wearing the spotless white garb of the highest Brahmin Hindu caste stood in the doorway.

"Can I do anything to help you?" Ida asked, noticing that the man's hands were trembling with anxiety.

"Oh, yes," the young man replied in excellent, cultured English. "I desperately need your help. My young wife, a girl of only fourteen, is dying in childbirth. The barber woman can do nothing for her and says she must die. I had heard that you have come from America and I thought you might save her!"

"Oh, no!" Ida said firmly. "I am not the one you want. You need my father, the doctor. I don't know anything about childbirth. I'll go get him."

"You don't understand," the young Brahmin said. "No man outside my family has ever looked upon her. No man, even a doctor, can tend to my wife. She will have to die."

"Oh, no! Please wait here!" Ida cried and ran to her parents' bedroom. She brought her father back to the young man where they both reasoned with him to change his mind to let her father save his young wife.

But the man shook his head sadly. "Then you will not come?" he said softly to Ida, turned and walked steadily out the door.

"I just don't understand," Ida cried to her father.

"It is because it would violate his caste law, and he is a very religious man and feels he can't break it. We must respect that. You already know that," he gently reminded her.

Ida went back to her room and tried to finish her letter to Annie. She knew about the religious philosophy of Hinduism and had visited the *zennas* (the women's quarters in Indian homes). They had shocked her. These women lived most of their lives behind four walls stifled by custom and culture. How could she explain this to Annie.

About an hour later Ida heard another cough and knock. She flew to the door thinking that the young man had changed his mind and come back to get her father to save his laboring wife. But to her surprise a different young man, a Muslim this time, dressed in a long, buttoned coat and white brocaded cap stood wringing his hands in the doorway.

"*Salaam*, Madam. May Allah give you peace. Please can you help me? It's my wife. She has had other children, but this little one won't come out. The midwife has given up and I'm afraid she will die. Will you come?"

Ida was stunned. This couldn't be happening again. "Wait here!" she cried and brought her father out to speak with the man.

"You don't understand our ways, Sir and Madam," the young man said. "Only the men of our immediate household can enter a Muslim woman's apartment. It is you, Madam, to whom I come for help.

"But I can't help her. I'm not even a nurse. I don't know anything about childbirth, absolutely nothing. I'd be glad to help you if I could!"

"Then my wife must die," the man said resignedly. "It is the will of Allah."

In an effort to comfort his distraught daughter, Dr. Scudder told her, "Forget! If there is nothing you can do to change an impossible situation, it is the part of wisdom to forget it."

Back in her room Ida tried to read her Bible but she couldn't concentrate. Finally, exhausted, she lay down on her bed staring at the ceiling.

Suddenly she heard another cough and knock. She was sure her mind was playing tricks on her frazzled nerves. Opening the door she saw a third, lower caste local Hindu man standing with tears running down his face. It didn't take long for him to blurt out the same, dreadful story. His child bride was dying in childbirth.

Sadly he turned and left when Ida told him she couldn't help him. She didn't even bother to wake her father.

There was no sleep for Ida Scudder that night. As the gray dawn appeared she heard the funeral drums. She sent a servant into the village to find out what had happened to the girls. "I am sorry, Madam," he said. "They are all dead."

Ida's mind whirled. Her father had told her to forget. But how could she? She thought of her dreams of college dances and a happy home with a husband and children. Could she give it all up to get the medical training she would need to save the lives of women dying from a lack of female doctors in this foreign country? But she knew the answer. She could never live with the thought of those three girls on her conscience, dying and doing nothing about it. She simply could not and would not forget them. Glancing at the letter to Annie sitting unfinished on her desk she realized in an instant that her vows to never serve as a missionary seemed shallow and selfish in the light of the last, life-changing night. Shaking the weariness from her body, Ida squared her shoulders and walked into her parents' bedroom study.

"Last night," she announced, "God sent me a message. I'm going to America to study to be a doctor so I can come back here and help the women of India!"

Postscript

Ida Scudder went to America and graduated from Cornell Medical School in the first class to graduate women in 1900. She returned to India and founded the first medical school and hospital for women in India in 1902. Dr. Ida became one of the most famous women of her day earning the Order of the British Empire. Her small hospital and school grew to become the co-educational Vellore Christian Medical College and Hospital, today one of the premier medical centers in India. Her niece, Dr. Ida B. Scudder, followed in her aunt's footsteps. She trained as a doctor and founded the radiology department at Vellore CMC & H serving there for over thirty years. Annie Hancock joined Ida in India as a missionary.

Ida's grandfather (and the author's great-great grandfather), the original missionary Dr. John Scudder, visited Mt. Holyoke College in 1843 preaching a sermon encouraging the students to become missionaries to bring the Christian faith to India. Although Ida Scudder was never able attend the seminary two of her nieces, Ida B. and Frances as well as her cousin, Susan Cochran Swanson, graduated from Mt. Holyoke. The Indian connection with Mt. Holyoke continues to this day.

The Carver
by Mary Dicker

Gloria Hansen, Public Health:

We were tracking him. Case G84. He'd had the disease for a year. We could tell even from a distance he was going to be all right. If we didn't lose him, he'd be okay. If we lost him, well who could tell. The disease would get him or something more sinister or mundane.

He was different from the others we tracked. No one spoke his language. We certainly didn't. It was an ancient language, indigenous. He spoke some English, some Tagalog, some Spanish, some Hawaiian. Like a man who's been on the seas, hauling in big fish, used to hardship.

When Carly approached him he looked right through her. Don't look him in the eyes I said to Carly. We don't know his culture. I don't think it mattered. His vision was impaired, clouded. She greeted him in her usual breezy manner. He was a man. Sure he would hear a young woman's voice. He turned his head towards her voice instinctively, but you could tell he didn't see her. It was the sound waves that drew him like the current in the seagrasses bending the stems in unison.

His hands were busy carving. His knife fit perfect in his hand, five inches with a wooden handle, blackened with sweat. His nails were split, fingertips splayed and clubbed, a sure sign of tuberculosis. His skin was the color of fallen leaves. The shape of the carving had not yet emerged. Chips landed on the pavement where he sat and on his shoes. His shoes were beat up, the backs smashed down. He wore no socks.

I nudged Carly. Speak to him, I said. Then we can mark him off for the day. She frowned at me. She didn't like me to tell her what to do when we were in the field. Her lips were chapped where she'd been biting them. I knew the texture of of her rough lips, how the scratchy surface felt against my ear.

Mister, she said. We didn't know his real name. It's Carly, she said, from Public Health.

He didn't look up. I know, he said.

You didn't pick up your meds this week, she said.

He waved the knife in the air.

Busy, he said, busy with the bird.

Can you make it to the clinic tomorrow afternoon? Carly asked.

Sure, he said, me and the bird, we'll stop by, he said.

Okay, Carly said. We're counting on it. He sort of snorted halfway between a laugh and a cough.

Don't you think we should know his real name? I asked. Try again, I urged Carly.

I see you're a carver. Is that your name maybe? Is it Carver?

That's dumb, he said. At least you tried, I whispered to Carly.

Carly Kowalski, Public Health:

Gloria is my colleague, my partner, and my lover. We are together most everyday doing our job.

When the carver didn't show up at the clinic, Gloria and me went back the next day and the next. To his spot by the freeway overpass. He didn't have any competition that we could see; no one muscled in when he wasn't there.

On the third day he was there sitting on the railing, hunched over, carving. His hand curled round the knife like a shell hiding its treasure. We came down the hill towards him.

I was first down the hill. Gloria held back. Later, she said something like: I saw you in your black boots and leather jacket. You blended into the harshness of the city. She thought I thought I was invincible. She thought I was fragile!

Gloria:

You know how for a second you know something is not right? You are thinking about a lover's faults, the scars of her life etched on her face, how she doesn't read the newspapers but still knows what's happening and your mind is off on its own trajectory. Well, that's how it was. I didn't see what was happening until Carly started to run.

Before the shots came, the carver was standing up. He was about five foot six. He had his carving knife in his hand. He was swaying back and forth on those smashed back shoes muttering some kind of nonsense in a language we would never identify. The cop's car was in the middle of the street with the driver' side door open. The cop was squatting aiming the gun at the carver. Then the carver was down and all hell broke loose.

Carly started to run. I grabbed onto her jacket. She kept on running down the hill, past the cop until she reached the body of the carver. I could've told her it was hopeless. He was dead. She wasn't going to save him.

The aide car came, a crowd formed, police cars cordoned off the area. Just like in the movies.

Carly:

I don't know why I ran to him. Instinct maybe. It seemed like the right thing to do. I'm a nurse. Gloria tried to hold me back. You could've got hurt, she said. He was dead. It was hopeless. All this negative shit.

His body was warm. He smelled like old alcohol and smoke. He was dead. I uncurled the knife from his grasp and put it in my pocket. I don't know why. No one saw me. I didn't tell anyone, even Gloria.

We had a smoke in the alley. I'm a witness, I said. I saw it all go down. I couldn't control the reaction of my body, the shivering, my teeth clattering. Yeah, Gloria is like, but that's not what's important. It's what kind of witness are you? Are you the right kind of witness? She actually said that.

So crazy. What did she mean was I the right kind of witness? She doubted me. Which is a grave thing when the world is not on your side.

But I had the knife in my pocket. I couldn't save him but I could be a witness. That knife was no weapon. I knew that was the truth.

Let's go back tomorrow, she said, We'll find the carving. That's dumb, I said. The cops are everywhere. They'll find everything, I said.

Gloria:

I told Carly she was wrong. I didn't mean to insult her. She was acting odd, distant. It was the trauma of finding a body and of seeing violence first hand.

They won't know where to look, I said. Yeah, she said, maybe they won't find what they're looking for. Her eyes widened and flashed.

I would do just about anything to tie Carly to me forever. She was like some kind of spirit goddess to me, some kind of drug, some kind of fetish. Like alcohol was to the carver. Like fashioning some kind of symbol out of rough wood until it had a shape and a meaning. And you would never let it go.

We went back the next day and climbed over the railing onto the dirt hill above the freeway. The police had been here. Boot prints indented the wet soil. The sorry details of homeless encampments littered the ground. But I was sure I could find the carving. Not on the ground but higher up, maybe in the blackberry thickets or in a tree, someplace you would hide a treasure, knowing just how priceless it was.

Carly:

We looked everywhere. I believed Gloria. I thought we would find the carving. I thought we would find the carver's blue heron. She described the bird to me as if it were a real thing with a wingspan made to skim the sea, a crest that ruffled in the wind. But the carver had let it go and it existed now only in some kind of ideal bird universe.

After that Gloria didn't tell me anymore how to do things. She stopped second- guessing me. I don't know why but I think it was because the years of experience between us didn't matter any more. Because I was older in some way. Because I had seen an innocent man shot and dying in the street.

You know what I mean?

Story
by Greta Climer

I wasn't careful on the way up
I rushed; I raced
I used my heart like a muscle
I lusted to tell the summit story
The Story of Us
How mighty we were
What we did with ease
With perfection

I wasn't careful on the way up
I had my eyes on the top
Didn't glimpse the view
Nor the obstacles in our way
I kept us moving, moving
Forward, up, upward, forward
Despite a need
A need to reflect, to relate, rejoice

I wasn't careful on the way up
I forgot it's the journey
Forgot it's the connection
Forgot that each moment
Each step
Is all there is
One moment—that moment
That is all

We are careful on the way down
We are living a new story
The Story of Our Truths
How human we are
How the path must be hard
How we aren't perfect

We are careful on the way down
We don't know where the trail leads
But we have learned
That resting matters
Relating matters
Rejoicing matters

We are careful on the way down
We treat our hearts like vessels
We love our journey
We nurture our connection
We cherish each moment
One moment — this moment
Is all there is

Untitled 1
by Greta Climer

It lies in front
And far behind
Showing neither beginning,
Nor how it unwinds
My path, it changes,
It matters not how
For all that does
Is this now

Untitled 2
by Greta Climer

My map didn't work; I got so lost.
That detour? The prize, not the cost.

The Difference Between Grief and Mourning

by Darla Willis Kennerud

The difference between grief and mourning is inconceivable and insurmountable and inevitable. It is an impossibly empty ecosystem in a bitter ocean, an echo with its own tides and moons. It answers a rhythm you had forgotten. To a child of five, or ten, or fifty, the gulf is as wide as the line is fine.

The difference between grief and mourning is the day you realize you will never make them happy and the day you decide to stop trying and the day you realize you never did. It runs forward forever, never back. You think it should run backward, but you can't quite see how. You will try to work on that, when you remember that you have forgotten.

The difference between grief and mourning is as private as the shame burning inside your stomach so hot that you spend the day waiting for combustion. Then maybe it would all make sense.

The difference between grief and mourning is as public as the burning bush of your body as it bursts into flames right there in the open. Everyone stares, gaping and dumbfounded, with the fire reflecting in their glassy eyes. It is not the way you thought it would be.

The difference between grief and mourning is the thing that changed your life being woven into your story generations before you were born. You are unsure why your lineage should matter to the three blind crones, but that is not for you to say, so you bite your tongue. You do this a lot.

When you start swallowing words, the difference between grief and mourning is the sharp, gingery space between the *i* and everything else and the buttery lowing of the *o-u-r*. Tears slide from your eyes, perhaps, but when you touch them with the tip of your tongue they have no flavor. Like you, they will not last.

The difference between grief and mourning is the abyss of a synapse, the neuron that fired one millisecond too late to make a difference. Around it goes, with the fire burning but the forge cold. The sword of Truth is a lump of unformed metal.

This Circle of Hands
by Mary Ann Woodruff

This circle of hands. . .
we pause before the feast
to look around us. . .

For nearly half a lifetime
I've stood in this circle
at this time of the year,
smiling into eyes that smile back,
marveling at the Grace
that brought us together.

Together, we've weathered
losses too deep for words,
marriages that turned to dust,
concerns and joys of family,
belly laughs and flashlight tag,
challenges of aging.

Together, we've watched
each other's children
stumble, bloom, become adults.
We've cheered their successes,
listened to their dreams,
encouraged them to follow their passions,
provided safe landing no matter what.

And the grandchildren!
They make us chuckle with their boldness,
weak with their energy.
They strike pleasure in our hearts,
often leave us breathless
with their talent.

This circle of hands
holds all of this and more—
our collective history and future—
for which, together,
we pause to breathe
our grateful Thanks.

How I Got Here
by Mary Ann Woodruff

If you ask me how I got here
I might shrug and say, search me;
I might say
life's a mystery;
I might say
I walked through some open doors
and not others;
I might say
now and then I get a glimpse
of the other side of my life's tapestry,
the side away from the slubs,
knots, and loose threads I see most of the time,
and that when I do,
I sometimes think I see a pattern.

But all of these would be half truths.

The truth — I know this now —
is that I was drawn,
as sure as the full moon pulls the tides,
to the shores of this vast ocean
and that her depths, swells,
rages and exquisite calms
are home to me.

If you ask me how I got here
I say I took a turn one day
and headed home.

Afterword

The Angled Road began in the fall of 2013. The Emily Dickinson Museum, in Amherst, Massachusetts, had held a session on how Dickinson had hand-sewn her poems into groups called "fascicles." We saw this session posted on the museum's Facebook page, and felt drawn to the remarkable low-tech publishing method. With the publishing world chasing its own tail these days, Dickinson's method seemed calm and fitting for her poetry. Why not bind our work that way, honoring it, tending it, putting hands to it?

Because of the Mount Holyoke College Puget Sound Writers, this idea began to "dwell in possibility," as Dickinson says. Our enthusiasm around the idea of creating our own collection, inspired by a poem by Dickinson, seemed to spur us on. Quickly, we chose our inspiration, delved into the poem, and created a statement of purpose:

The primary purpose of this project is to create something together and document the process, to teach us about creativity and marketing, journey from concept to public product and to expand our personal and public identity as writers.

The Angled Road project asked us to strengthen our skills intensely, as writers, readers, editors, and revisers. We made many convoluted but democratic decisions together. On our web site (mhcpugetsoundwriters.com), we blogged about our process. We handled a sample fascicle in the Amherst archives, and bound one of our own. We devised an innovative system of reader response. We were respectful of each other, but we also challenged each other. We surprised ourselves with the vibrant collection of notably varying pieces. We held a reading, sharing our work more widely. An unexpected gift came our way through this project: we were invited to be the guests of the University of Washington's English Department at their event, Ten Takes on the World of Emily Dickinson.

The Angled Road pushed us further than we had planned on going. Our project's road was itself angled, revealing to us our next curve at the same time we tried to chart its full course. Very little, with our Angled Road, felt "predetermined" — at least predetermined by us.

In the end, we had to let go of imitating Dickinson's art and use a more modern, less time-consuming method of publishing our collection — which you hold in your hands. We've made one fascicle as keepsake rather than commercial venture — which perhaps honors the original spirit of Dickinson's efforts better.

—Emily Dietrich

The Contributors

Teri Kieffer Bicknell '89

In my spare time, I write short stories and novellas; by day I work for a small software company that serves nonprofits. I will never forget my first visit to Mount Holyoke. Late afternoon sun lit up the elegant nooks and crannies of the Highway 116 side of the Rockies. A woman passed by, smiled at me, and said, "Hi." I felt completely welcomed, and the experience remained that way throughout my years there and beyond. I have experienced the same welcoming inclusion as a member of the MHC writing group, and I'm grateful to feel that kinship and connection again.

Elizabeth Burr-Brandstadt '91

I have spent my years since Mount Holyoke as both a teacher and a student. After teaching high school English for almost 15 years, I moved from the East Coast to the West Coast to start a new chapter, which included marriage and earning a PhD in Mythological Studies with a focus in Depth Psychology. Meeting other Mount Holyoke women and specifically participating in the writing group has been a joy for me, and has also encouraged me to explore my voice as a writer. Even though I now live in the Seattle area, Mount Holyoke will always be close for me; my education there continues to enrich and inspire my life.
• http://thresholdsofculture.com

Greta Climer '91

Being part of our Mount Holyoke writers' group is like every other MHC experience I've had: nurturing, inspiring, stimulating, challenging, and invigorating. Mount Holyoke continues to grow me in so many ways and will never cease. I am grateful for the connection and community of our amazing Mount Holyoke writing group!

Mary Dowd Dicker '66

I am so grateful for Marjorie Kaufman, Professor of English Literature, who taught me how to read. I joined our local Mount Holyoke writers' group hoping to find support and inspiration for my own writing (fiction, poetry). I'm currently living on an island not far from Seattle but far enough to find a slower pace of life and beauty all around.

Jules Dickinson '77

My original reasons for selecting Mount Holyoke had nothing to do with women's education but I've come to realize that this college, and its being a women's college, was likely the most valuable experience I've ever had in my journey towards becoming a person. I joined this writing group in part to learn from others, their thoughts and their writing, so that I can become a better poet. I use poetry to help me get in touch with and express my feelings and thoughts; any improvement I can make in my writing experience improves me.

Emily Dietrich '85

I'm the author of *Holding True* and am currently working on my second and third novels. I loved walking back to the Mandelles in the fall, kicking leaves, thinking big thoughts, feeling aware, awake and alive. I started this writing group in 2013 and have been pleasantly surprised at how satisfying it has been. Making new Mount Holyoke friends wherever I've lived, I continue to benefit from my experience there, and expect I always will.
• http://www.magentic.org
• http://www.facebook.com/emilydietrichauthor

Darla Willis Kennerud '89

I work as an editor in the game publishing industry and am the mom of two kids. I've had writing published by *No Quarter Magazine* and, more recently, Skull Island eXpeditions (skullislandx.com). Although I've been a writer since childhood, I've always struggled with balancing that part of my life with my role as an editor, and before that, an advisor. I worked in the Mount Holyoke College Writing Center (as it was known then) for three years and loved it, but I never worked with MHC women on my own writing. Older and hopefully wiser, I'm grateful to have that opportunity now. Whether light-hearted or soul-searching, discussions with MHC women are exhilarating, inspiring, and thought-provoking!

Sue Cochran Swanson '60

Mount Holyoke gave me the confidence and skills to first realize and then strive to reach my potential. I joined the MHC writing group after meeting them at Mary Ann Sparklin Woodruff's book launch party. It's been fabulous. Meeting with this group of intelligent, fun, and supportive group of MHC grads has been like inhaling a long, cold drink after crossing a desert.

Mary Ann Sparklin Woodruff '60

I wrote *The Last of the Good Girls: Shedding Convention, Coming Out Whole*, in 2013. Its cover image is from my sophomore year in Sycamores, an off-campus Mount Holyoke dorm housing fifteen lucky women. Pledges from an Amherst fraternity came to serve us at a "gracious living" dinner, and we got gussied up for the occasion. The MHC writers' group has been both an inspiration to me to keep writing and also a barrel of fun sharing our lives and writing together.

• http://www.facebook.com/Mary.Ann.Woodruff.Author

Krista Lee Johnson '85 *(cover artist)*
I chose Mount Holyoke because it had horses and a great art program — but declared my major as economics! Thank heavens I listened to the incredible women around me my freshman year. I was soon studying classical guitar and immersed in studio art classes. I spent my junior year in Italy, and after college I spent four and a half years at an atelier studying the painting and drawing techniques that I so admired while in Italy. Much of my work is portraiture; my commissioned installations include Children's Hospital of Minnesota and several large churches in the Minneapolis area.
• www.kristaleejohnson.com

Acknowledgements

We appreciate the time, effort, and expertise of Roy Leban. He designed this volume and managed its production. We thank him sincerely.

Made in the USA
Charleston, SC
03 October 2016